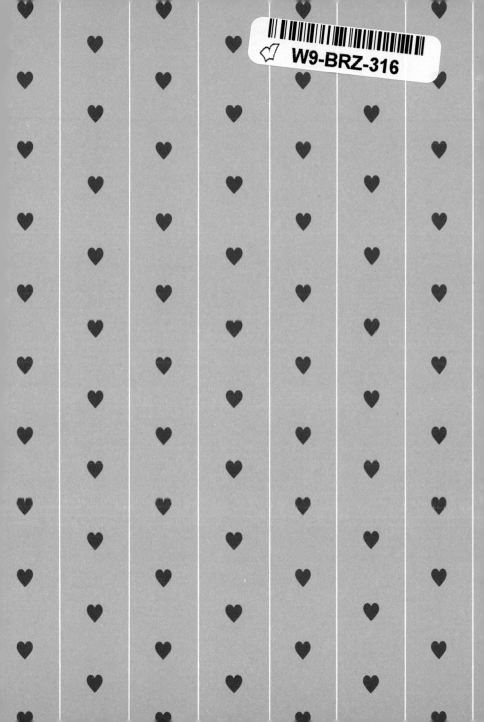

W9-BRZ-316

BALCONY PEOPLE

BALCONY
PEOPLE

From the Heart,

JOYCE
LANDORF

WORD BOOKS
PUBLISHER
WACO, TEXAS

A DIVISION OF
WORD, INCORPORATED

BALCONY PEOPLE

Copyright © 1984 by Joyce Landorf

Library of Congress Cataloging in Publication Data

Landorf, Joyce.
    Balcony people.

(From the heart)
    1. Christian life—1960–   2. Rejection
(Psychology)   I. Title.   II. Series: Landorf, Joyce.
From the heart.
BV4501.2.L31815 1984   248.4   84–11866
ISBN 0–8499–0378–5

Scripture quotations used in this book are from *The Living Bible,*
copyright © 1971 by Tyndale House Publishers, Wheaton, IL.

"In Other People's Shoes," reprinted by permission from
Lift My Spirits, Lord by Bryan Jeffery Leech,
copyright © 1984 Augsburg Publishing House, Minneapolis, MN.

Printed in the United States of America

*I was hungry and you formed a humanities club
to discuss my hunger.*
Thank you.

*I was imprisoned and you crept off quietly
to your chapel to pray for my release.*
Nice.

*I was naked and in your mind you debated the
morality of my appearance.*
What good did that do?

*I was sick and you knelt and thanked God for
your health.*
But I needed you.

*I was homeless and you preached to me of the
shelter of the love of God.*
I wish you'd taken me home.

I was lonely and you left me alone to pray for me.
Why didn't you stay?

*You seem so holy, so close to God; But I'm still
very hungry, lonely, cold, and still in pain.*
Does it matter?

—Anonymous

♥

Linda's scissors were making their usual precisionlike snipping noises around my head. "Where are you going this time?" she asked.

"Dallas."

"Ah, *Dallas.*" Linda's marvelous smile flashed at my reflection in the mirror. I knew she was remembering the last time she'd been in Dallas. Linda had done my hair and makeup during the filming of my *His Stubborn Love* film series. Since she had never attended one of my seminars or speaking engagements, or any *other* Christian event for that matter, the "Dallas experience" had been anything but what she had expected! God's timing was perfect that day. And the Lord used the filming to touch Linda's life on the deepest level possible. She's not been the same since.

"Are you speaking in that same church?"

"No, this is for the International Convention of Christian

Booksellers. I'm the speaker for the Thursday night banquet at the close of the convention."

Linda continued cutting my hair. Then, after a few more minutes she asked, "What are you gonna talk about?"

"The gift of affirmation."

Linda's scissors stopped abruptly. She looked at me in the mirror again, tilted her head to the side, and said with a straight face, "That's great! What's affirmation?"

Good question, I thought. *There's so little affirmation in the world today we hardly know the word, much less understand the concept.*

"Let's see." I tried to sound brilliant. "Affirmation is one person affirming another."

Linda's blank look went from "You're kidding" to "Okay, I give up."

I began again. "Actually, Linda, affirmation happens when I come into your shop to have my hair done, and, since I *know* you are going to work a miracle on my hair, I verbalize my appreciation and gratitude. I *affirm* you when I say, 'Linda, you're incredible! I bring you my oily, straggly bunch of fine, reluctant-to-be-tamed hair, and you work your brand of magic on me! I leave your shop clean, combed, and *almost* gorgeous.' My words affirm and assure you of my love for you as a person, my confidence in you as a professional hairdresser, and my belief in you as a person of value."

She looked at me for a second, snapped the hair dryer on, and smiling with comprehension said, "I like it!"

And I thought to myself, *Don't we all?*

We like it when those we know and love communicate their

admiration for us by making positive comments about us based on their respect, and we like it when they verbalize their love for us. (Personally, I love it!)

This book is about the lethal poison of rejection, and the healing antidote of affirmation.

Affirming someone because we respect their human worth and personal dignity is a rare and lovely thing. But affirming someone because of the bond of God's love between us is downright marvelous!

The bonding process between Christians is spectacular—different from those in the world. I can turn on the radio and feel "loved" by Neil Diamond's love song "Hello, Again, Hello," but there is no *genuine* affirmation. Godly affirmation is based not on what we are, or what we've accomplished, but just on the fact that we are *who* we are. For instance, there is an incredible bonding which happens almost instantaneously when a doctor puts a newborn infant, still wet from the birth canal, upon the mother's bare breast. The mother affirms her baby not for what the infant has accomplished or achieved but simply because the baby *is*.

The early Christians were the first to experience this bonding process, and they changed the world with their love. Paul and many of the New Testament writers knew that our spirits could soar to unlimited heights on the wings of another's affirmation. Conversely, they knew that our spirits could plummet and shatter when hammered by the blows of criticism or rejection. So they spent considerable time writing on the need for us to affirm each other.

When others discern the good, the noble, the honorable, and the just tenets of our character (no matter how minuscule they may be) and then proceed to tell us how they admire those traits, we feel visible. We begin to "see" ourselves and our worth. We feel nurtured and nourished, but mostly we feel loved.

Why in the world is affirmation such an undeniable need in our lives? What is the matter with our self-concept that causes us to continually need to have our sagging spirits shored up like the buildings along the canals in Venice which sink into the water a few more meters each year? Must we be complimented on everything we say or do, hour by hour? Why do we long so desperately for approval and appreciation from the people who touch our lives?

I never understood this perpetual need in your life or mine until I started actually researching letters and interviews for my book *Irregular People*. It was then I came face to face, over and over again, with people who had been given massive dosages of *rejection*. I came to believe that the average human being is inundated with rejection, in varying degrees, from birth to the end of his or her life. What's more, I discovered that the rejection I'd experienced during my childhood and adult life was no big deal. In fact, rejection is not the exception, but rather the rule.

After hearing me speak on the subject of affirming, a woman who signed herself only as "a friend," wrote these words,

> Dear Joyce:
>
> Thank you, thank you.
> You understand and express

a woman's truth.
How wonderful it is to know someone
else understands.
Keep speaking to us.
Keep reminding us how much God
loves us.
We need that love, not the constant
judgment we pour on ourselves.

Yours truly,
A friend

Her words, "the constant judgment we pour on ourselves," point out that rejection (sometimes the severest kind) comes not only from others but from within as well. Finding genuine affirmation and real expressions of love is as tricky as it is rare. We run into rejection with ourselves, others, even special loved ones. And we find it at times when we least expect it! Rejection is found *everywhere*—in homes, schools, stores, businesses, even airports.

Once when my husband, Dick, and I were changing planes at the airport in San Francisco, we ducked into the gift shop just long enough for me to find two greeting cards. The clerks were frantically busy, but I eventually reached the counter and gave the cashier my money. After she had counted back my change she immediately turned and waited on someone else, forgetting to give me a bag for my cards. Since she was already ringing up the next sale, I held up my cards to another salesperson standing in front of me. "I've paid for these," I explained, "but I need a bag. May I have one?"

I'll never forget the clerk's look of utter disbelief. It was as though I'd asked her to give me the keys to her car. She just shook her head no and, making no move to the bags, which were stacked under the counter within easy reach, she cryptically said, "It's not my shift yet."

I discovered in that moment that you can experience rejection at the hands of someone you've never seen before! Dick and I just stood there and laughed. I never did get a bag for those cards.

Months after that marvelous lesson in humanities, whenever I asked *anyone* in my family to get something or to do something, I was most likely to hear, "It's not my shift yet." Around our house that line was good for about three years of laughs.

Before we understand how to be affirmers, we have to face the reality of rejection and its lethal force in our own lives. We need to deal with our own brokenness in order to move out into the world as affirmers. ♥

THE SPARROW

Resilient and swift with winged endurance,
Undaunted by raging storms,
Remarkably agile, vigorous and strong.

Yet fragile if snared and too tightly grasped,
For then, crushed and broken lies
His body, his spirit, and his song.

—M. H.

♥

As I write about our relationships with others, our expectations of our own gifts and abilities, and our perception of both these subjects, I have about concluded that there are only two basic types of people in the world: *the evaluators and the affirmers.*

I *am* sure, if there were a way to view a movie and see instant replays of all the strategic change points in our lives, that we'd instantly spot the people who either broke our spirits by their critical or judgmental evaluations, or who healed us by their loving, perceptive affirmations.

To be honest, I seem to be able to remember the negative comments of evaluators faster and more clearly than the positive remarks of the affirmers. I'm not alone in this ability to recall the negative, as immature as it is, for many of you have verified that you, too, think along those same lines. I suspect that not far from anyone's conscious level of thinking lies the memory of an evaluator who pulled on his or her spiked boots and stomped deliberately over our bare soul and personhood.

As I grow older, however, I am learning (slowly) that I have a choice about evaluators—past and present. I can choose to keep them and their judgmental opinions in the *past,* even if the "past" means just yesterday.

A very insightful woman, writing me about the book *Irregular People,* discovered this same choice about evaluators. She had been irritated by a remark made by a woman in her family, and she wrote,

> I told myself I would not let it get to me. But I soon found my mind playing her words over and over—imagining myself repeating them to my husband, daughter, and a person with whom I work. The Lord broke into my thoughts with His quiet voice and said, "Those words [from the woman] came to pass—why don't you *let* them pass?" And I had to agree it was true. If I would just let what she says and does "pass with the doing and saying" and not keep them around by mulling them over in my memory, it would be much easier.

We all have the choice to replay the harmful remarks from evaluators, or we can choose to let them pass on. We can even choose to make allowances for their discouraging, destructive words. But best of all is the choice to willingly focus our minds and hearts on *today's* person who is *affirming* us.

Let me ask you. Who is the affirmer in your life, who by one small sentence or more, has *changed* and *lifted* your opinion of yourself? Who was the person early in your life who recognized the first sparks of originality in the labyrinths of your mind and soul, and saw what no one else saw? And who is the special affirmer who catches quick glimpses of the flames from the fires of your potential and *tells* you so? Who, by his or her words, helps you to respect and believe in your own value as a person? And who is the affirmer who encourages you to stretch and dream beyond your self-imposed limits and capabilities?

Whoever these people may be, I know their name, for they are called *Affirmers,* with a capital *A.* I have known only a few genuine affirmers, but one affirmer is worth a thousand evaluators.

In my childhood my chief and constant affirmer was my mother, Marion Miller. She called me "Joyce honey" even on the days when I was not *exactly* honey sweet. She was a planter of dream-seeds, and died before she ever saw the harvest of her plantings.

My affirmer in the fifth grade was a music teacher named Mrs. Applegate. She told the entire girls' glee club that when I grew up I'd be a famous singer.

When I was eleven, my affirmer was the songwriter extraordinaire, Audrey Mieir. She told my mother that when I grew up I'd be a famous pianist.

At sixteen, the composer and thoroughly unique Phil Kerr, affirmed me by allowing me to sing in his Monday Nite Musicals with all the number one "biggies" of the Christian music world. Phil, however, told me that when I grew up, I'd be a famous writer. (By then I didn't care about being a famous *anything,* I just wanted to grow up.)

In my midtwenties, when I had become a wife and mother, there was a whole string of incredible women who became my affirmers. There was Henrietta Mears, Velma Spencer, Dale Evans, Melva Wickman, Gert Behanna and of course, as always, my mother. These women had one thing in common: they were all rich and famous in God. It was as though each one's lifework and occupational priority was solely to affirm others, and in doing so *they* each gained great wealth of spirit themselves.

One of the best things about these affirmers was that they helped me to discover and see myself by a clearer, truer light. They were always able to peel back the layers of pretense I wore like costumes for a bad play. Most of the time they saw through *and* past the masks I hid behind. Then, once having broken through to me, they'd get on with the business of motivating me to be all that I *could* be. Because of these women (and later, other affirmers in my life) I've learned much about my true identity in Christ. I even found I liked some (not all) of the traits in my character.

It was my mother who, early on, discovered the insatiable levels of my curiosity, and my fertile imagination. She set herself to teaching me how to see and hear everything that was going on around me. (It was training that I use every day of my life now, as a communicator.) It was also then, while my mother was developing my ability to observe the smallest detail, that I discovered I was deeply attracted to tiny things. To me, less is more.

For instance, I love observing with all my senses a dainty,

fragile-looking little girl or a three-year-old boy who mimes his dad's actions so much that he looks like a miniature man. I am charmed by a yellow kitten who looks like a small sphere of golden fluff sleeping in the sunlight or a soft brown-eyed puppy who begs to be hugged. I like to listen to a lone musician sing a cappella or play a violin. I appreciate a single pearl, a solitaire diamond, a rosebud, a tiny translucent sea shell, a petite blue-purple butterfly. But, most of all, I am particularly pleasured by watching a tiny, spirited bird . . . especially a sparrow.

When I was thirty years old, knowing my love of music, tiny things, and my gift of imagery, my mother gave me the book entitled *Jenny Lind, The Swedish Nightingale*. She inscribed the front page with, "To my little sparrow, who can sing like a lark." I was thrilled by the story of Jenny Lind, but I was totally enchanted by being called a "little sparrow."

Four years later, when my mother died, I leafed through all the Bibles and books she had given me. The chill of her death was somewhat warmed by reading her affirming comments. But none eased my heart quite like the inscription calling me her "little sparrow." She knew I loved tiny things and that my imagination could easily visualize a mother bird lovingly caring for her baby offspring. Her words were always an original and different way of saying "I love you."

I have, on a rare occasion or two, spoken about sparrows and my fascination with tiny things, but for the most part of my public life I've kept this facet of my thought processes to myself. So I was more than a little taken aback last year, when a woman

I'd met only casually a few times asked, "When are you going to write about the little bird?"

Thoroughly stunned, I finally managed to respond, "What bird?" and wondered how she knew. How could she have so accurately read my mind or seen so directly into my soul?

She reached over to me, touched my face gently and said quietly but distinctly, "The tiny bird who lives *inside* you. You know, the one that is so broken it cannot fly or sing anymore."

She knew. The woman knew! I thought I'd kept that little broken bird well hidden, but here she was asking me to write about it. My astonishment must have been written on my face because she asked, "Don't you know about small birds?" I shrugged my shoulders. She responded, "Then let me tell you about them."

For the next few minutes she gave me a detailed, almost scientific, description of the life and times of a small bird, such as a sparrow.

Sparrows, she told me, possess remarkable strength and endurance records. They seem to be impervious to severe winds or inclement weather. They fly continually, all day long, foraging for food. They have been clocked at great speeds and have been known to fly hundreds of miles during one daylight period. Their endurance and energy levels are enormous, and even their wing revolutions per minute present an awesome number. Sparrows are incredibly strong and tough little birds, making them appear virtually indestructible.

When my new friend had finished her discourse on the sparrow's amazing strength, she looked at me and continued softly, but more intensely, "However, as powerful as sparrows are, if you, as a human being, were to catch a sparrow in your hand and squeeze it, you could break every bone in its body and crush it to death within thirty seconds."

She waited while her words formed pictures in my mind, and then, still gently, she said, "You are very much like a sparrow. You *appear* powerful, strong, impervious to the storms of life, but I see you are crushed and broken, without a song. And I have to ask, who has crushed you?"

I couldn't speak. She sat down across from me and almost as if it were to herself she whispered, "You are a strong, powerful lady. Your audiences and readers draw great hope and courage from your life's examples. You are resilient and seem undefeatable, but you hide the fact that you have been broken and that your song is gone. Someone has reached down inside of you and crushed the life out of your heart. When will you write of this? When will you admit the damage and try to sing again?"

For days after that encounter, I wept. How well I knew of the little bird lying broken and silent at the bottom of my soul. How familiar I was with the human beings who, by their critical or judgmental *evaluations,* had crushed my spirit and carried off my song.

You and I are absolutely no different. We have all, at one time or another in our lifetime, been crushed by an evaluator or two.

Yet, particularly as Christians, we are *expected* to appear victorious. We are *expected* to be on a continuous spiritual high. We are *expected* to fly, as the sparrows, undaunted into the storms of life. After all, aren't we God's children?

The dilemma forces us to put on our brightest smiles, and we give forth our most ebullient greetings when asked about our well-being. We hide the painful truth from ourselves and other children of God as though a crushed spirit represents a hideous flaw in our character. We deny that someone, even a saint of God, has caught us in their wrenching grip of words and has snuffed out our ability to shine. But mostly we deny that an empty void even exists within us for fear yet another evaluator will come along and condemn us or, worse, try to set us straight.

So we retreat behind masks. We feel hypocritical and have nagging feelings of guilt for what we know we are *supposed* to be, compared with the reality of what we are. But we feel safer behind our masks.

An intriguing piece, anonymously written, entitled "Please Hear What I'm Not Saying," bypasses our masks, our denial systems, and goes for the heart of the matter.

Please Hear What I'm Not Saying

Don't be fooled by me.
Don't be fooled by the face I wear
For I wear a mask. I wear a thousand masks—
    masks that I'm afraid to take off
    and none of them are me.

21

Pretending is an art that's second nature with me
But don't be fooled, for God's sake don't be fooled.
I give you the impression that I'm secure
That all is sunny and unruffled with me
   within as well as without,
   that confidence is my name
   and coolness my game,
   that the water's calm
   and I'm in command,
   and that I need no one.
But don't believe me. Please!

My surface may be smooth but my surface is my mask,
My ever-varying and ever-concealing mask.
Beneath lies no smugness, no complacence.
Beneath dwells the real me in confusion, in fear, in aloneness.
   But I hide this.
   I don't want anybody to know it.
   I panic at the thought of my weaknesses
   and fear exposing them.
That's why I frantically create my masks to hide behind.
They're nonchalant, sophisticated facades to help me pretend,
To shield me from the glance that knows.
But such a glance is precisely my salvation,
   my only salvation,
   and I know it.
That is, if it's followed by *acceptance,*
   and if it's *followed by love.*
It's the only thing that can liberate me from myself
   from my own self-built prison walls

from the barriers that I so painstakingly erect.
That glance from you is the only thing that assures me
of what I can't assure myself,
that I'm really worth something.

But I don't tell you this.
I don't dare.
I'm afraid to.
I'm afraid you'll think less of me, that you'll laugh
and your laugh would kill me.
I'm afraid that deep-down I'm nothing, that I'm just no good
and you will see this
and reject me.

So I play my game, my desperate, pretending game
With a facade of assurance without
And a trembling child within.
So begins the parade of masks,
The glittering but empty parade of masks,
And my life becomes a front.
I idly chatter to you in suave tones of surface talk.
I tell you everything that's nothing
And nothing of what's everything, of what's crying within me.
So when I'm going through my routine
Do not be fooled by what I'm saying
Please listen carefully and try to hear
what I'm *not* saying.
Hear what I'd like to say
but what I can not say.

I dislike hiding.
   Honestly.
I dislike the superficial game I'm playing,
   the superficial phony game.
I'd really like to be genuine
   and me.
But I need your help, your hand to hold
Even though my masks would tell you otherwise.

It will not be easy for you.
Long felt inadequacies make my defenses strong.
The nearer you approach me
The blinder I may strike back.
Despite what books say of men, I am irrational;
I fight against the very thing that I cry out for.
You wonder who I am?
You shouldn't
   for I am everyman
   and everywoman
   who wears a mask.
Don't be fooled by me.
At least not by the face I wear.

I will be eternally grateful for a woman who was not fooled by the masks I wore to cover my broken spirit. She looked past those masks and dared ask me to face and even write about the broken places of my life. Then, as a genuine affirmer, she let me know that having a crushed spirit and no song to sing was not a grievous sin, but rather a serious wound that would heal by God's hand and in His time.

The encounter with her, the story of the fragileness as well as the strength of sparrows, and the truths I faced that day have certainly caused me much soul searching. But I am more convinced than ever that if our inner brokenness is ever to be made whole, and if we are to ever sing again, we will need to deal with the issues of evaluators and affirmers in our lives. I also *firmly* believe that the need for *affirming one another* is crucial to our process of becoming real, not phony or hypocritical, people of God. Affirming brings authenticity and credibility to our Christianity as it is *lived* day by day.

I must be affirmed, and I must be an affirmer to others. Otherwise I miss one of the main concepts of the New Testament—to love one another and to bear one another's burdens. ♥

*Lord, is it You who would teach me
the distinctive differences between
evaluators and affirmers¿*

*Are the guidelines for being an affirmer
found in 2 John where it is written,
"If we love God, we will do whatever he
tells us to. And he has told us from
the very first to love each other."¿*

I think so.

*Then please, dear Lord, strengthen my
ability to understand and practice love.*

—M. H.

♥

Back in 1968 I understood very little about affirmers and evaluators, and I certainly had no idea of the great need in all our lives for someone to believe and encourage us. But in the summer of that year, on a Southern California beach, I met a man who was, and still is, a born teacher in the rare art of affirming.

It was vacation time and Dick and I had borrowed a small house trailer and were spending a week with our children at a State beach. During the days, while my family swam and rode the waves (I hate water that is cooler than 85°), I sat on the beach soaking up the sun, doing my favorite thing: reading.

I took a number of books, all with the hope that as I read them God would give me some inspiring guidelines which might develop or enlarge my own writing skills. I was at a point in my writing career when I began facing what I now know to be a rather typical frustration common to authors: a writer's mental block. My second book, *His Stubborn Love,* was going nowhere on my writing tablet. I didn't know what to leave in our testimony story, what to leave out, or even how much of our troublesome marriage I should reveal. I fervently prayed as we drove to the beach that God would dissolve the block between my mental abilities and my pen.

But of all the good and even great books I took to read, analyze, and study that summer, it turned out that I read only one. It was Keith Miller's *The Taste of New Wine,* and I was forever changed by the experience. Keith's words melted the formidable brick wall in my mind by giving me a clear awareness and a new sensitivity to *honest* writing. His book had a refreshing openness and candor that seemed missing from so many other Christian books I'd read.

Day after day I sat on the beach reading and rereading and analyzing the forthright style of this truly chosen man of God. I came away from this initial introduction to Keith's writing determined to pattern my own work on this type of candid authenticity. Besides underlining passages in the book and writing myself notes in the margins, I purposed to never settle for anything less in intent and attitude than Keith's high level of honesty and literary vulnerability. (Later, Eugenia Price's *The Burden Is Light* had this same kind of stimulating, inspiring, and freeing effect on my soul.)

Today when someone tells me how much they admire and respect the honesty in my books, or in my speaking, I am instantly reminded of who it was that gave me my very first glimpse of what honest communicating is all about.

For almost twenty years now I have read all of Keith's books, watched his progress in Christ, corresponded with him, and have become his friend. I have seen this man triumphant in his successes, awesomely humble regarding his literary genius, and broken and shattered in defeat by the sheer force of personal rejection.

In her book *Heart Held High,* Martha Snell Nicholson, another favorite of mine, wrote of broken people when she said,

> We are now His broken things. But remember how He has used broken things: the broken pitchers of Gideon's little army, the broken roof through which the paralyzed man was lowered to be healed, the broken alabaster box which shed its fragrance abroad and the broken body of our Savior.
>
> Let us ask Him to take our broken hearts and to press upon them *further* suffering to give us a poignant realization of the suffering of the world. Let us ask Him to show us the endless, hopeless river of lost souls. This will break our hearts anew; but when it happens, God can use us at last.

In recent years God, as the Master potter, has gathered up the fragmented pieces of Keith Miller's heart. He has taken Keith's shattering divorce and the stinging rejection from the body of believers which followed, and has molded and shaped the broken clay into an incredible vessel—a leader unlike other leaders, a communicator unlike other communicators, an affirmer unlike other affirmers, a man who knows the agony of brokenness and the overwhelming joy of wholeness, a man who is on intimate terms with God.

When I read John Fischer's great but unsettling book, *The*

Dark Horse, I could think of no one but Keith Miller. In the Introduction John explains:

> The dark horse has become a symbol of the ordinary person who comes out a winner due to the grace of God.
>
> But most importantly, the dark horse is an image of real Christianity . . . righteousness amidst human flaws.
>
> The church is inundated with white horses. Flawless, successful, inaccessible leaders who only drive the average Christian deeper into frustration, guilt and failure.
>
> If we are to learn to follow Christ, it will be the dark horses, not the white ones, that will show us the way.

But even knowing and loving Keith as I do, I was still not prepared for the specific way God would use this dark horse so beautifully to show me new ways of being His child. It is Keith who has shown me how valuable God's "darkening" process is to growth, and it is Keith who has taught me some very firm concepts and truths about affirmers and evaluators. The lessons are indelibly imprinted on my mind.

The strongest, most powerful lesson came in Keith's film series, *New Wine.* He severely rocked my snug, comfortable, little evangelical boat of theology with his dark-horse approach. This convincing and convicting series on the subject of our walk with Christ reached deeply into my heart and, as in the case of my 1968 experience with Keith Miller, he added greatly to my hope. My life was changed.

Word Publishing, producer of Dr. James Dobson's film series and several others (including mine), asked me to introduce the

Keith Miller films at the premier showing for the annual Christian Bookseller's convention. So, in order to speak halfway intelligently, I asked for and received the whole series on video cassettes. Then I settled down one weekend, while Dick was on a men's retreat with our church, to view all six of Keith's films. An illustration in the fifth film stopped me and gripped my heart like nothing had in a long time. I replayed the video tape of that film three times to let it all sink in.

At first I didn't have any idea Keith was talking specifically about affirmers and evaluators in our Christian life-experience. But gradually, during Keith's fifth film, I began to decide that when he was calling the church today an "outpost of the kingdom" he was talking about the very quintessence of Christians *affirming one another.*

He dealt with our need to relate to others on an honest, realistic basis, and our need for openness and confession. And as Keith wrote in *The Scent of Love,* which is based on the film series:

> We can't receive love personally as long as we are hiding our real selves. So, if the church is to become a place where individuals learn to receive love, we have to discover how (in a sensitive, nonthreatening way) each person can be "seen and heard." We must learn to be open to one another—"unacceptable" feelings as well as hopes and dreams—so that we can each receive the love and cleansing of God through his people.

Another characteristic of the church as an outpost of the kingdom of God, as Keith described it, was the believer's precious responsibility to listen and care *in the name of Christ.*

31

I have long struggled with Christians who have written me over the years during my bout with jaw and head pain, for so many of them gave me "unsolicited advice" or tried to "straighten out my program" with criticism. And most of the letters began by saying, "I tell you this in Christian love." How I thank God for the rare affirmer sent my way in the past ten years of hideous pain, who listened, cared, and gave me *no solutions,* all in the name of Christ!

In that fifth film, Keith talked of the church body listening and caring so expertly that church members would, in essence, *unwrap* another child of God to discover his or her true identity and natural God-given vocation.

I soaked in Keith's words like a hard, dried-up sponge, but when he began talking about the Freudian concept of our conscious and unconscious mind I was really, as my kids would say, *blown away!*

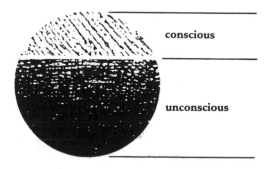

Keith asked us to envision our minds as if they were housed in a clear glass sphere or circle. The bottom two-thirds of the globelike ball is filled with the dark, murky water of our unconscious minds. The top third is filled with the pure, clear oxygen of our conscious mind.

Then Keith began talking about the people who live in the dark murky waters of our unconscious mind. They are family or friends, living or dead, who continually reach up through that black water, grab us, and pull us under. Freudian psychologists call these people "basement people."

The basement people of our minds pull us down with comments like, "You're not gonna make it." They tell us we *can't* do such and such. They drop subtle or not so subtle hints about our inferior qualities, and thoroughly damage our personhood. Perhaps it was a mother or father who verbally abused you, or pushed your head under water by what they did *not* say. Maybe it was a teacher who said, "You are so stupid, I can't believe it!" and instantly, she or he became your basement person. To this day you remember drowning in their critical evaluation.

"Basement people" came as a bunch of bad news which I'd already guessed and recently discovered because I'd been speaking on the exact same subject, and had just finished writing the book *Irregular People*. But then came the good news. Keith explained that the late Carlyle Marney, an incredible pastor, counselor, and theologian, said we Christians are different from the people of the world. Because along with "basement" or "cellar people," we have the extraordinary advantage of having "balcony people" in the top third of our minds.

33

Think of it! All around that sphere of clear air in our conscious minds runs a balcony filled with people who are not merely sitting there, but practically hanging over the rail, cheering us on. My imagination fairly exploded with the mental pictures.

Keith began telling of the balcony people in his conscious mind, some living and some dead, but all of them united in inspiring him and in making him feel he could be more than he was.

He named the Lord, Paul the apostle, David the psalmist, Andrea, his children, authors, and dear friends. Keith went on to say that just about the time he felt he was failing in something or about to go under because of the basement people of his life, he'd look up, and there a balcony person would be leaning over the railing shouting, "You *can* do it, Keith! I believe in you!" Their words would give him strength, courage, and a great surge of confidence, and he'd be saved from drowning at the hands of his basement people.

I sat spellbound, watching Keith and listening to his soft accent, and I was moved beyond words. His intense sensitivity to being alive in Christ and his "balcony people" concept overwhelmed me.

Taking out a fresh sheet of yellow, lined note paper, I wrote out a list of who was in *my* balcony. (I already knew who was in the basement, and I felt I'd given enough importance to them. It was appropriate to give equal time to balcony people.) My list of people included the Lord, Paul, David (Keith didn't have an exclusive contract with those men) and, to my surprise, there was the apostle Peter. Up to that point in my life I had not thought of Peter as one of my favorite people. Yet when I saw him there, in the balcony of my mind, cheering me on, I realized that over and over in the recent years in my battle with chronic pain, it was words like these that kept me going:

> This suffering is all a part of the work God has given you. Christ, who suffered for you, is your example. . . . Dear friends, don't be bewildered or surprised when you go through the fiery trials ahead, for this is no strange, unusual thing that is going to happen to you. Instead, be really glad—because these trials will make you partners with Christ in his suffering, and afterwards you will have the wonderful joy of sharing his glory in that coming day when it will be displayed. . . . After you have suffered a little while, our God, who is full of kindness through Christ, will give you his eternal glory. He personally will come and pick you up, and set you firmly in place, and make you stronger than ever (1 Pet. 2:21, 4:12–13, 5:10).

Yes, these words are from Peter—outspoken Peter who, after the transformation by the Holy Spirit, used his same mouth to be a gentle affirmer and great communicator. He was in my balcony, calling softly to me, during my hours of greatest pain.

My mother, already in heaven's balcony since 1966, was clearly visible. But unlike the others who were cheering me on, she (who had always told me I was special and that God would give me a unique ministry) just leaned over the railing, smiled, and shouted, "I told you so!"

I could clearly see that my family and a small but beautiful group of friends were in my balcony. Some had been there for a long time without my knowing it, and others were new to the cheering section. But they *were there.*

The writer of Hebrews tells us to run with patience the race that's set before us "since we have such a huge crowd of men of faith watching us from the grandstands" (Heb. 12:1). Ah, that "cloud of witnesses" in our balcony, past and present. What would we be without them?

After I listed *who* was in my balcony, I was a little surprised at how few people were present. But then it seemed to me that it's not the amount of people, but the high caliber and level of credibility that really counts. After all, it only takes one "basement person" to drown us in the murky waters of failure and discouragement. Why not then, the reverse? It only takes one "balcony person" to lift us up and restore our sense of well-being.

Listing the people who were in my balcony, I concluded, was only half of what should be written. So I got out another sheet of paper and put down all the names of people to whom *I'd* be a "balcony person." Finally, I decided I'd given absolutely enough attention to the basement people of my life. It was time to concentrate on my balcony people and on *being* a balcony person to others. ♥

LAMENT

Oh, Lord, I feel so worthless, inadequate, a nothing!
  Prove me wrong!
Lord, I feel so unloved, unlovable.
  Send me someone who will love me deeply,
  So deeply that I can believe otherwise!
I feel so alone, so lonely, so empty.
  Fill me up; surround me with Your presence.
I feel no one cares, no one needs me, no one wants me.
  Please, God, prove to me that I am wrong.
I feel forsaken, blocked off, locked out of joy.
  Oh Lord, Lord, don't You have the key?
Words seem so empty, no weapon against the lonely pain.
  Lord, make Your promise of love come alive for me!
I cannot see You;
You are so distant, so omnipotent, so supreme.
I cannot believe that You could care
For such an insignificant me!
  Please God, show Yourself to me
  So I can really see
  And feel and touch and hold You.
  Show me You in a human, so I may know the reality

That I can see and touch and hold.
I want to hurt myself, ridicule myself,
Wound myself in their presence
  So they—and You—may pick me up,
  And soothe me and comfort me and make me feel loved.
I want to scream and cry and catch someone's attention
  So others will start to care,
  So others will want to stop me,
  So I can see that it makes a difference . . .
  NO! . . .
  That I make a difference in their lives.
Oh God, I hurt so, I want so;
I hunger and thirst to be Somebody
To Somebody who is important to me.
You are sometimes not real enough,
Not tangible enough to hold on to.
Then Your promises seem like whispers lost on the wind.
And the blessings I have felt seem to melt
From my memory and from my assurance,
And are mere illusions, no longer a foundation for faith.
Oh Lord, I feel lost.
  Please find me.

Search for me and seek me
So that I can really believe that You want me!
Oh God! Is it only a dream that I felt loved?
I can't feel it now!
I can't touch it now!
Love is the only life-line that will save me;
Yet I sink deeper down the abyss.
Oh God, reach out, with human hands and human
    words and human love
And hold on to me with divine love
And don't let me go!
I'm so afraid of never having had it at all.
    Oh Lord, my God, please prove me wrong!

—Marcia Esther Allen
(Used by permission)

♥

The woman who wrote the preceding "Lament" was, as we all are, in great need of a balcony person. How well she knew her need.

Once I heard a Catholic priest I know and dearly love speak about the relationships we have with other believers. He said, "As Christians we should live in relationships with people in such a manner that even when we leave a room people will miss us. And when we are gone, and our funeral is held, someone will cry . . . someone will deeply miss us."

Last year I attended the funeral of just such a man. Ray De-Vries, the former vice-president of special services at Lexicon Music/Light Records, had died of a heart attack at the age of fifty. At his funeral Ralph Carmichael, who gave the eulogy, told of the life Ray had lived . . . he called Ray his "pastor" and the "corporate conscience" of Lexicon and Light Records. But what impressed me the most, was at the very end Ralph, with tears streaming down his face, said simply, "Ray was my friend, and *I'm going to miss him.*"

It wasn't that Ralph didn't know he'd see Ray in heaven one day . . . it wasn't that Ralph denied Christ's victory over death, it was simply that Ray's life was so incredibly lived that the human side of Ralph (and of all of us who loved Ray) would *miss* the man.

It was Ray DeVries's kind of Christian life my priest-friend was talking about when he said, "In order to have this special kind of relationship with others, we need to be gentle, peaceful people, and we need the power of Jesus' love." Following this statement my friend then asked four questions:

1. How do we form these kinds of relationships?
2. How do we become keenly attentive to each other?
3. How do we become really *present* to each other?
4. How do we relate to others so that it makes a difference?

My friend answered his own questions by saying that Jesus was so present to the woman at the well that He could perceive her need. He gentled her, and she found herself drawn, convicted, and so changed that she ran to the town to tell everyone to come and meet Him.

The priest expressed it beautifully when he said,

Each of us has a weakness from which we run, a love which we hesitate to share, a need to receive, a need for the growth of gentleness, a need for the fact of reconciliation.

We are at times fragile needing support; weak needing strength;

frightened needing assurance; lonely needing companionship; isolated needing other believers; sinful needing forgiveness and grace; fearful needing the calming love of God; sick, worn, burned out needing a healing.

When I heard him say these words I thought, *Oh, how desperately we need to look up in the balcony of our minds. We need to see and hear the Lord and people who by their presence and their words lift our discouraged spirits and urge us onward in the race we run. For, "we are at times, fragile."* ♥

IF YOU CAN TALK—I CAN WALK

Once I was a dancer—
  Taking lessons in New York.
Once I was a skier—
  Challenging the mountains of Montana.
Once I even walked.

Joints retire after 100,000 miles—especially a congenital
  hip.
It seems, my friend, that we've worn out
  The very hinges that have supported us.
So if you can talk—I can walk.

Keep talking (and writing), sister.
  So that all will truly know
  That the miracle lies in the talking and the walking.
  That pain we can endure only if Jesus is there—

He will help us along the way
By crying with us.

You have touched me . . .
    And I am changed
It's okay to be in pain—
    It knocks the rough edges off fast—
As long as there is someone to cry with—
    Someone to hold onto when the pain gets worse.
Jesus—so abandoned in His pain—is ever-present.
And it is such a blessing to know there are people—
Especially two very dear people—I watched from the
        balcony
Who know how powerful and revealing
    That pain can be.

                    —Jeanette Murphy
                    Balcony Person Extraordinaire
                    (Used by permission)

♥

The early Christians of Rome, Corinth, and other New Testament places, were undoubtedly the first balcony people. Their love was so astounding that a first-century *pagan* wrote, "Behold, how these Christians love one another!"

How did they "love one another" and really become balcony people to each other . . . those early Christians?

I think it was something they were taught. And I also believe that loving in the name of Christ did *not* come as naturally to them as breathing. For if Christian loving and affirming were an easy thing to do, why then, are the writers of the New Testament so loquacious on the subject? Probably because then, as now, we must be taught the art of loving; someone must nurture us, and thereby we *learn*.

The characteristics of balcony people are varied. You can probably come up with a great many more than what is written here, but I'd like to give you just three traits which true balcony people learn and give away—they love, listen, and care from the heart.

BALCONY PEOPLE LOVE FROM THE HEART

Recently hundreds of people wrote me after hearing a broadcast on pain which I did with Dr. James Dobson, but one woman's letter ended with this poignant line, "We hold your hand in love and *softly* cradle you in our arms of prayer."

She brought a gentle healing to my soul as her love was so obvious. Did you notice that her words were framed in as much unconditional love as humanly possible? She offered me no solutions or advice, she wrote without criticism or judgment . . . she just loved me, and told me so.

The early Christians were taught to be balcony people and to truly love others. Their teachers were Paul, John, James, Peter, and other writers of the New Testament. Above all else, these men taught *love*. Christians were not to love as the people in the world around them loved, but by a special God-placed love and in the name of Christ. They were to be a set-apart people with a set-apart love. This brand new teaching was verified by all the writers. Clearly we read, "If we love God, we will do whatever he tells us to. And he has told us from the very first to love each other" (2 John 1:6).

Loving each other, affirming each other, and being balcony people means there is no room for criticism and judgmental attitudes.

Listen to James as he says, gently, "Don't criticize and speak evil about each other, dear brothers. If you do, you will be fighting against God's law of loving one another . . ." (James 4:11).

And Peter as he states, "So get rid of your feelings of hatred. Don't just pretend to be good! Be done with dishonesty and jealousy and talking about others behind their backs" (1 Pet. 2:1). He also says "Show respect for everyone. Love Christians everywhere" (1 Pet. 2:17).

And Paul admonishes, "Don't just pretend that you love others: really love them" (Rom. 12:9). "Love each other with brotherly affection and take delight in *honoring each other*" (Rom. 12:10, italics added).

When balcony people love, they *do* take extraordinary delight in "honoring each other." They are *not* in competition with each other, and they particularly do *not* keep score.

It seems to me that few, too few, of us honor one another. We are too interested in our own welfare, our own successes, our own achievements. We are intimidated by someone else's gifts or talents. We become so busy climbing the ladder of our own triumphs that we resent taking the time to pay homage to someone else.

True balcony people love with honor and respect.

In the sixteenth chapter of Romans, Phoebe was described as a dear Christian woman. Paul tells the church in Rome to "receive her as your sister in the Lord," giving her a warm Christian welcome." Then he goes on to advise, "Help her in every way you can for she has helped many in their needs, including me."

Paul continues to teach the balcony people concept by

example when he writes next, "Tell Priscilla and Aquila 'hello.' They have been my fellow workers in the affairs of Christ Jesus. In fact, they risked their lives for me; and I am not the only one who is thankful for them: so are all the Gentile churches."

Later, in that same chapter, Paul says, "Remember me to Mary, too, who has worked so hard to help us." Paul has no trouble being a loving balcony person to women, nor does he struggle in the least with respecting Priscilla, Mary, and other women for their work in the church. In fact he comes right out and calls them co-workers. I suspect several women were partners with Paul in the Lord's work, and I do *not* mean they cooked and served the Wednesday night potluck supper.

The entire sixteenth chapter of Romans is, in my mind, the biblical "balcony person" passage. It is where Paul practices what he preaches. He cheers all those dear people in Rome from the balcony of their minds. He gives no false compliments, no build-up of one person and belittling of another; but straight from the balcony, he gives his love.

My favorite balcony motto from Paul is that marvelous sentence, "Whatever you do, do it with kindness and love" (2 Cor. 16:14).

Another trait balcony people learn is the ability to really hear others.

BALCONY PEOPLE LISTEN FROM THE HEART

Real affirmers are always searching for ways to improve their hearing. Evaluators are always talking.

It's strange, but I think it's just part of our human nature to be more comfortable with evaluating than with affirming. The truth seems to be that we *love* being evaluators and basement people. Somehow we think that by offering our advice or opinions, we will look intelligent and blessed with uncommon wisdom. Yet being a true balcony person and a dedicated affirmer is *vastly* different. Balcony people listen and then, instead of tearing down others, they build them up.

Sometimes we are called to be evaluators. (Notice, I did *not* say we are called to be basement people.) Mothers, fathers, teachers, pastors, men and women in the legal and medical professions, and many other people are all evaluators of different sorts. However, even when we are put into the evaluator's role, we will only bring wholeness when we approach evaluating from the balcony position. Also, in our role of evaluator, if we do not precede our evaluations with affirmation, it not only becomes useless rhetoric, but it can be destructive to the point of being eternally damaging. Balcony people know listening is just as important as loving!

The other night a dear friend called me at my home. I was tired, irritable, pressured by a missed deadline on this book; and while I was not hostile, I was uncharacteristically quiet and unresponsive. My balcony friend picked it all up, and in a long letter which came the next day, she poured out her heart. I knew she'd really *heard* what I was feeling because she wrote,

> One thing that's nagging at me is a most unsatisfactory, incomplete feeling about our phone conversation this evening.

I know my timing wasn't ideal—dinner waiting, you were with others, schedules pressing in, etc.—and that *may* explain all of it.

But . . . I'm really searching for words now . . . there was a depth of the *unspoken* there, a depth of where you are, that we seemed to be skirting or touching only with polite formalities. Oh, I did hear between the lines . . . I don't mean that we didn't *say* things—

But I was left with a sense of being ready for a steak and walking away with celery sticks.

I wanted somehow, tonight, to communicate to you that I *do* really understand where you are . . . I have tasted your pain and know that I am qualified to sit at its table with you. All I ended up saying was that I would come and walk or sit with you and that you could say *anything* to me.

But I wanted you to know that you are free to be open. I wanted you to hear my heart and know that I'm not into passing judgments.

I can't! For I have met my own humanity, and it in turn has introduced me to understanding, compassion and, most of all, a willingness to learn.

Tell me, do I seem to be asking for your friendship or your time? I am not. I know that we are already friends and that you *have* no time.

I think I'm asking for an invitation to a place that has no name. It's a place that I *must ask* for an invitation to attend, for it's a place I would *never* go *un*invited, and yet—I wait to attend.

The closest I can come to explaining it is to say that I'm waiting for an invitation to that raw place of need in you (and in me), that unnamed bastard of ourselves that is surrounded by flashing yellow signals . . . that place that gasps with unqualified reason

and then aches with unpronounceable pain at the loss of a rare and unexpected find . . . that place where hope goes to die . . . that place that stubbornly refuses to allow our dreams to unite with reality and be satisfied . . . that place where self-esteem and ego struggle to change robes in the dark.

Oh, precious Joyce, I sit here at midnight knowing that I have never made myself more vulnerable, knowing that I ask for this admittance, offering the gift of myself, not in response to my own need to be known, but at the unpracticed measure of your need.

And there is something *else* I know about such need and such pain . . . sometimes it *withdraws*. Sometimes it seems unable to do anything else. If you are there . . . well, I understand.

You need to know that my love is not based on your seeing or doing things my way!

I will *always* love you.

My friend, in the truest sense, is a skillful listener and one of my dearest balcony people. But what touched me deeply was that she wrote the content of the letter not from what she *heard* me say, but rather, what I *did not* say.

It is a longstanding dream of mine to hold workshops to train lay people (particularly women) in the lost art of listening.

One of the most severe problems facing a pastor of a small or medium-sized congregation is the number of hours he must spend in counseling sessions. His church probably cannot financially employ a staff counselor; so, upwards of 80 percent of the pastor's time is spent counseling on a one-to-one basis.

If we could train lay people to listen to others without evaluating, without criticizing, without giving disapproving looks,

and without handing out condemning and judgmental state-
ments, I believe we would bring about two powerful types of
healing: (1) lay-listeners would free the pastor to study, preach,
and teach; and (2) lay-listeners would perform a scriptural and
deeply needed ministry with hurting hearts.

I am not suggesting that we don't need trained and highly
qualified counselors and psychologists. On the contrary, *we do!*
However, as close as our backyard there are hurting people who
are desperately longing to have someone listen to them. There
are people everywhere who, right at this time in their lives, need
someone to listen and to be supportive. Someday, my dream
will come true, and balcony people will be able to listen to what
others are *really* saying, and the ministry of these listening hearts
will be incredible.

The balcony person who poured herself out to me in the
preceding letter has much to teach us all about listening from
the heart. She has caught the true ambience of listening. Her
lines, "I'm not into passing judgments. I can't! For I have met
my own humanity" tell us much about her creative powers to
listen without presuming, assuming, or judging.

Our son Rick has an outrageously funny laugh. We absolutely love it. In fact our whole family just breaks up the very
first moment Rick starts to laugh. The students in the high
school where he teaches science refer to him as the teacher who
has the "Woody Woodpecker" laugh; and they tease him con-
stantly, which of course only makes him laugh harder.

When I hear Rick's laugh, I cannot tell him to quiet down. I
cannot be embarrassed or offended. I cannot be critical and tell

him to refine or change his laugh. I cannot be judgmental and suggest his laughing is all wrong, or that his laugh is undignified. Know why?

Because I've heard *myself* laugh.

Once we come face to face with our own imperfections, our own limitations, and our own *humanity,* we have little room to talk about someone else's. And once we begin to fathom the truth that God does not hold us accountable for anyone's actions or thoughts but *our own,* we can use this knowledge to help enlarge our capacity for heart-listening.

Listening requires that we face and understand our own fragile and complex ways. It means too that in view of our own humanity we see others in a different light, and when we listen to others we make allowances for them—as we would have them make allowances for us.

Paul instructs us in Ephesians to be humble and gentle, and then he tells us who would listen from the heart, "Be patient with each other, making allowance for each other's faults because of your love" (Eph. 4:2).

I'm sure I wouldn't understand as much about "allowances" if it were not for a pair of jeans I now own.

All my life I've had at least one friend who wore jeans and who made the wearing of jeans sound like the next best thing to a religious experience. Someone was always saying, "I could just live in these jeans!" And, ever since I turned fifteen, I've been going to stores, trying on jeans, and *never* finding a pair that fit or did not bite and scratch me, much less one that I felt I could just "live in."

A few years ago when designer jeans were introduced I thought, *Aha! Now these jeans will satisfy my urge to "live in jeans." They will be cut differently, they are made of more expensive fabric, and perhaps I'll know exactly what this frantic, basic love for jeans is all about.* But, alas, while the designer jeans didn't bite or scratch, *I* still looked bad . . . well, more like a little lumpy. (I was hoping for something closer to a cross between Victoria Principal and Nancy Reagan—but it didn't happen.)

I can't tell you how often I've tried on jeans, to absolutely no avail. But, not too long ago, my friend Mary Jean Bhatt was waxing eloquent about the wonderfulness of jeans, and so I decided I'd go to a store just one more time. The next day, while I was in a Gemco discount store, I saw a whole rack of designer jeans. I tried several pairs on and . . . *nothing.* Then, just as I had given up and was leaving the store, I spotted a rack of no-name jeans. The third pair I tried on fit! It not only fit, it felt great! I still looked a bit lumpy, but the jeans were so comfortable I quickly rationalized myself out of my insecurities.

All the way home I was dying to call Mary Jean and tell her about my "find." All the way home I also wondered *why* the jeans fit and felt so good! Later, as I was cutting off the labels and price tag, I read these brief words: "95% cotton and 5% Spandex."

"So that's it!" I shouted. "Spandex! Five percent Spandex is what makes the difference. That stretching flexibility given to the threads makes it possible for the jeans to go in where I go in, and to go out where I go out." The jeans were perfect! And suddenly I knew why we have such a problem listening to others and making allowances for them. We don't have 5 percent Spandex in our attitudes. Without being disrespectful, I'm sure that had Paul known of Spandex the Ephesians verse would have read, "Be patient with each other, making [a 5 percent Spandex] allowance for each other's faults because of your love."

In evaluators, the listening mindset is generally fixed at 100 percent something. But, I'll tell you, when someone is *listening to me,* I definitely want them as an affirmer to have at least 5 percent Spandex in their attitudes and thinking.

Affirmers, balcony people who love and listen from the heart, do so with much Spandex; and, consequently they hear between the words.

BALCONY PEOPLE CARE FROM THE HEART

Affirmers are always interested in finding ways to care for others. Evaluators care, but only for their own interests, their own advancement, and their own successes. Real balcony people are simply fantastic in their ability to pick up the baton of "bearing one another's burdens," run with it, and really win the race.

One such affirmer in my life is Francis Heatherley, executive vice-president for Word's publishing division. I have watched him as he finds creative ways to care for people. I'm blessed to be a close friend of his, but I am stunned at his skill in caring for many, many others.

I've known him for a few years now. I've watched him in

action, and I stand in awe of his remarkable ability to bring out the very best in so many authors, members of his family, and even in people who, to my way of thinking, are fairly unlovable. His gentle North Carolina accent, his quiet demeanor, and his extraordinary ability to love, listen, and care, are not hoarded up within him. They are not stingily doled out only to a select few. He lavishly spends himself on behalf of others—*all* others.

"How do you do that?" I asked. "What's the secret philosophy behind your brand of caring?"

He answered me with a very heavy statement, and I had to think it through before I fully comprehended. He said, "The best man in the world is the man who helps himself, and the only way to help one's self is to help others."

When I finally worked through Francis's remarkable adage, I remembered three men in an interesting parable told by Jesus. But now I saw them by a different light. One was a Jewish priest, another was a Levite who was a Jewish attorney-type for the temple, and the third was a wealthy but despised man from Samaria. All three had some degree of success, credibility, and wealth. All three saw the naked, almost dead man beside the road. But only one cared. The other two stepped around the man's bleeding body and went on their way.

They were evaluators. Perhaps they reasoned that their work was of more importance than tending to the man's wounds. Maybe they felt "time was money," and their schedules too pressing to be interrupted or halted. I can only guess at what they thought, or what their line of reasoning was in leaving the man to slowly die. But I am sure that after they gave the situation their evaluation and came up with the results of their "quick and dirty" study, they simply did not *care* enough about the man to help him. Oh, I think they *cared*—but not enough to *act.*

The Samaritan was a dark horse—a man who not only saw the need of another person and cared, but actively set about to *help.* He gave verbal, nonverbal, financial, and physical care to a needy victim.

The Samaritan was, in Jesus' opinion, *the best man.* I know that was our Lord's opinion because in Luke 9—the chapter just before the Good Samaritan Parable—Jesus was in the midst of dealing with the disciples' humanity. (I love Scripture because it does not paint unreal pictures of people. It shows their beauty *and their flaws.*)

The disciples were, of all things, arguing among themselves about *who* would be the greatest in the coming kingdom. The Lord read their minds, and gave them and us a special lesson. He stood a little child up in front of them and announced His criteria for greatness, and the *best man* award, when He said, "Anyone who takes care of a little child like this is caring for me! And whoever cares for me is caring for God who sent me."

Then Jesus gave His men the formula for being *the best man.* He said, "Your care for others is the measure of your greatness."

Think of that! *My* care for someone else is the measure, the determining factor, the depth, the magnitude, and the very touchstone of *my greatness.*

Francis Heatherley's words—"The best man in the world is the man who helps himself, and the only way to help one's self is to help others"—come alive when I truly understand the biblical concept of caring.

Balcony people care from the heart, and their ability and capacity to care is a measure of their greatness. ♥

IN OTHER PEOPLE'S SHOES
Romans 12:15

*Lord, your love increases my sensitivity
to needy people in today's world.*

*I bring my prayers to you:
for those who suffer pain;
for those whose minds are disturbed;
for brilliant people who waste their abilities;
for those with great potential
    but who lack the opportunity to realize it;
for those whose dreams have shattered;
for those who live behind bars;
for those who have been maimed by violence;
for those who have been disgraced and wounded
    by other people's wrongdoing;
for those who have lost a loved one;
for those who are suffering from incurable diseases;
for those who face death,
especially those who face it without you.*

*Help me, Father, to make myself available
to those who need help,
that in practical and in spiritual ways
I may convey your love to them.*

—Bryan Jeffery Leech

♥

Often I've wondered how we could change our world, the countless relationships that we encounter, and the agony over a lifetime if . . . if only we were balcony people to each other. I have a very active imagination, and I love imagery, but my mind boggles a bit when I think of what would happen if we actively, not passively, pursued the balcony concept.

BALCONY PEOPLE IN MARRIAGE

Just yesterday a letter came to our offices and a young woman wrote, "I thought you should know that you saved a marriage. My aunt and uncle, who were seriously considering divorce, heard your 'Balcony People' tape and after years of putting each other down (verbally) decided to stop it and become balcony people to each other."

In a marriage it's easy to take each other for granted. It's easy to grow accustomed to our partner's talents or gifts. It's easy to neglect the praising of their good points. It's easy to slip into belittling our mate and thinly disguising it by calling it humor. It's easy to be unkind because, after all, we don't have to perform or be on our best behavior with those closest to us. But those "easy" patterns are the most destructive in the world!

I am one of the directors for Azusa Pacific University's School of Theology, and at a dinner the other night husbands and wives were asked to introduce *each other*. What a *refreshing* time that was, for I heard *men* say, "This is my wife, a wonderful, patient mother to our two sons, and the absolute *joy* of my life!" Another man said, "This is my wife, my lover, and my business partner. She is the greatest salesman in the world, and probably will pass out contracts to everyone here before we leave. She's the smartest woman I know. I love and respect her with all I have!"

There were no "basement" remarks; and it was marvelous to see husbands and wives being balcony people to each other. The love, the respect, and the admiration were not phony, cute, or hypocritical, but warm, genuine, and extremely Christ-like.

BALCONY PEOPLE TO IMMEDIATE FAMILY

You only have to read a few samples of the mail I receive on *Irregular People* to get an accurate picture of how parents and children cancel out each other with "basement people" attitudes. Only eternity will tell how many souls have been truly damaged by the rejection that's felt between parents and children in families.

Whenever I go to the grocery store, I'm reminded that I used to turn from a nice person into an absolute tyrant when I had to do grocery shopping with my young children. That memory helps me to understand why mothers can go from mere animosity to deep hostility while shopping with their kids.

Mothers must be evaluators who dispense discipline, training, answers, and transportation, while at the same time providing food, clothes, baths, and clean sheets. Yet, to evaluate those little ones *without* affirming can be deadly.

After hearing me speak on this subject at a meeting in Kansas, one darling young couple told me, "We wanted our daughter (four years old) to be so perfect we had become strict evaluators; we are going to change that. We've decided to love and affirm her, as well as be her evaluators and, like your mother did for you, we are going to tell her how special she really is." Those parents have just taken their first steps toward being *real* balcony parents.

A short word to teenagers here. Perhaps if *you* decided to become a balcony person to your mom or dad (*regardless* of their human flaws) *you* could end up with a tremendous measure of greatness.

I only wish I'd known this balcony people concept years ago when I had little ones, but now that I'm a grandmother to four precious cherubs I've a second chance, and I'm going for it with all my might!

BALCONY PEOPLE TO EXTENDED FAMILY

I wonder what changes would occur in the lives of in-law parents, brothers, sisters, cousins, and other relatives if we stopped trying to settle every score and discontinued our efforts to straighten out everyone else's life?

Honestly, I know there are some *impossible* people out there— I'm related to a few myself. But hear me, this is a plea from my heart: Criticism and judgmental pronouncements rarely *change* anyone. It's only God's incredible love, *through us* as balcony people, that has been known to work miracles!

BALCONY PEOPLE ON THE JOB

I enjoyed the allegory, *The One Minute Manager*. The authors tell us in the Introduction that they are writing about how people can work best with other people. I identified with many of the principles set forth in this little book because I saw balcony people concepts in many lines.

Think what *could* happen to our relationships with other people in the work place if we put into practice the affirming traits of balcony people. Now granted, there are some basement-people types and overbearing evaluators in *any* job, but I'm suggesting that *we* take the responsibility to be affirmers to the people around us.

It doesn't matter whether we are waitresses, doctors, sales clerks, truck drivers, librarians, opera singers, or mailmen . . . we can be affirmers. We can do this whether in management or labor. And although I believe that affirming is one of the most effective (yet subtle) ways of spreading the good news, it also enables us *to work best with other people.*

When I first saw the Keith Miller series, remember I said I wrote out two lists. One named the people in *my* balcony. The other named the people to whom *I'd* be a balcony person. The first name on the latter list was my former pastor, Jim Rehnberg. I wrote him a long letter, telling him all about the concept of balcony people, and that I'd committed myself to cheering him ever onward! "You preach, I'll turn the pages!" I now know my letter came during one of the most difficult times of his life. And before the year was up he had resigned his pastorate. My letter reached him the same week four couples left our tiny sixty-two-member church (they said he wasn't "feeding" them), and my dear pastor read my letter as he was about to die from pulpit despair. Pastor Jim was not touched because my letter was clever or brilliant, but because *God* used the words to bring a healing. But God could not have used an *unwritten* letter.

What would happen to our churches, or to the body of believers, if we decided to zipper our mouths against negative, hurtful, or egotistical pronouncements and give ourselves to the *exquisite,* rewarding task of affirming?

I have an oversized burden for pastors' wives and children. Perhaps it's because I'm a P.K. (preacher's kid) and I *lived* in church during my growing-up years.

Recently I spoke at a luncheon for over five hundred pastors' wives. Outwardly they looked beautiful, bright, and spiritually believable. But as I looked inside their eyes, I saw their immense loneliness; I felt the chill of their discouragement; and I knew the aroma of rejection which clung to their skin like a pungent perfume.

Most of us do not allow our pastor and his wife to experience *any* marital strife or discord.

We do not allow a pastor to admit or deal with depression when it attacks him unmercifully, as it did Charles Spurgeon for all of his life.

We do not allow a pastor the permission to be angry, to be human, or even to grieve for a death in his family.

We do not allow a pastor's wife to have mental illness, emotional burn-out, or even a miscarriage. She *must* be spiritual at all times, with a handy biblical reference on the tip of her tongue. She must never have a bad day and lose her spirit or her temper, and most of all she *must* be able to play the piano.

We do not allow pastors' children to grow, to develop; we make no allowances for their immature humanity. Their fishbowl existence makes them an evaluator's dream target.

When will we stand beside and behind the man of God who, for this time, is chosen to lead; and when will we hedge our pastor about with loving affirmations?

If we ever do become balcony people of God to our ministers, you'll know it instantly. There will break out over pastors, missionaries, lay people, and congregations alike, the greatest revival the world has ever seen!

BALCONY PEOPLE TO BELIEVERS

Could it be that we have rather carelessly glossed over a whole spectrum of believers in our churches who desperately need the practical application of the balcony people concept? There is a rapidly emerging group of believers which includes single people, divorced people, single parents, young adults from unchurched backgrounds, people who are struggling with their sexual identity, senior citizens, handicapped people, and parents of the handicapped. But there are also people in homes, businesses, schools, hospitals, courts, government . . . people in all walks and modes of life, who are a part of our spiritual family. What of them? Are they not *you* and *I* . . . and do we not need the lifting of our souls by a balcony person?

Oh yes! Yes! ♥

I wrote My purpose into you . . .
It is My song you have to sing . . .
I gave it to you with love.
In your fear,
You think you have your own song . . .
that the idea to sing
is your own
and that the music depends on you.
You are My precious child,
And before you were even born,
I had you in mind—
And I am the One who wove the
lyrics and the melody
into the fabric of your life.
So, My child,
sing My song.
Let the music flow through you with freedom . . .
as My love
and power
flow always through to you.
And don't forget . . . The song in you is My idea.

—Jeanie Miley
(Used by permission)

♥

My little grandson James was two years old and visiting me in our backyard one summer day. I was talking with his mother (my daughter Laurie) and James was deeply immersed in his little cars and trucks. He happily stayed that way until he heard what, to him, was a very frightening noise.

I knew it was the big garbage trucks rumbling down the street to pick up our curb-side trash barrel. But James knew no such thing. It was a sound he'd never heard before, and it scared him right out of his little socks. By the time the truck stopped in front of our house and put on its screeching brakes, James, who could not see the ferocious enemy, was panic-stricken.

He looked up to me, as I was the nearest adult, and with his big blue eyes opened to their widest capacity he fairly yelled, "Hug! Hug!" And the look on his face screamed, "Hurry! Hurry!"

I remember reaching down for him and wallpapering his little body to my chest. It was a long time before he moved, and even longer before the color came back into his face. I've never forgotten the moment.

It seems to me that the noisy pandemonium of this evil world is exploding all around us like cannon volleys. We are desperate to be hugged—to be rescued, to be home safe. We are shouting through our panic, "Hurry! Hurry!"

What is the frightening noise in your life?

Is it the noise of cancer, divorce, rejection, discouragement, depression, loneliness, or something so terrible it shouts but remains unnamed? Whatever is pounding loudly in your mind, your body, or your soul, let me be your balcony person. Let me hug you with my words. Let me wallpaper your soul to mine. Let me encourage you to sing God's song, and let me remind you that the song in you is His idea.

Hear me when I say the apostle Paul did not lie when he wrote, "Long ago, even before He made the world, God chose us to be His very own." You and I are His children. I believe in you. I'm leaning way, way over your balcony railing; I'm waving my coat above my head, and I'm yelling above the frightening noises of your world, "I *love* you! I *believe* in you and your abilities! You *can* do it! Keep at it. Keep on! God chose you before He made the world, and you know what? He's here beside me; yes that's right, He's here, and He's not sitting down. You are His child, He is your Father. His coat is off too, and we are both in your balcony cheering you on together!" ❤

ABOUT THE AUTHOR

Joyce Landorf is known nationwide as a uniquely gifted Christian communicator, able to convey biblical principles with relevance, humor, compassion, and conviction—in a way that speaks to the needs of men and women in all denominations. A bestselling author of both fiction and nonfiction (her 19 books include *Silent September, Irregular People, He Began with Eve, His Stubborn Love, Mourning Song, I Came to Love You Late, Joseph,* and *Changepoints*), she is also an immensely popular speaker and conference leader. Her *His Stubborn Love* film series, based on her nationally acclaimed seminars of the same name, was the recipient of the 1981 President's Award from the Christian Film Distributors Association. Joyce and Dick Landorf reside in Del Mar, California.

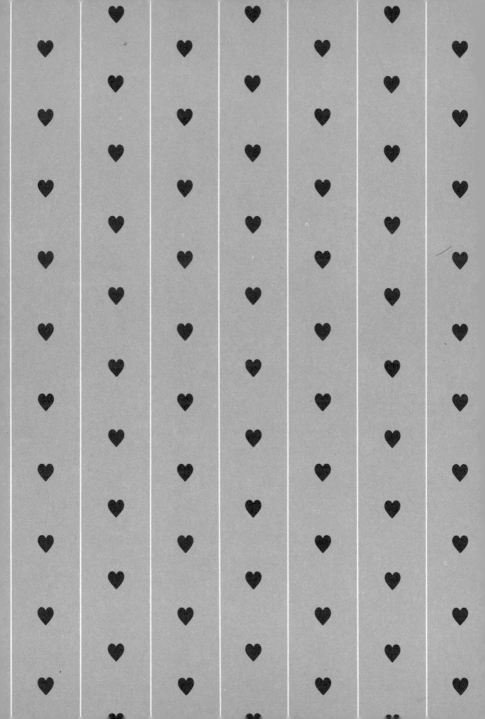